I Can Fly®

Reading Program
Book B

By Cheryl Orlassino

Blast Off to Learning Press

For information, apps, phonics tools and chapter books, go to

www.BlastOffToLearningPress.com

Go to www.ICanFlyReadingProgram.com for the web app.

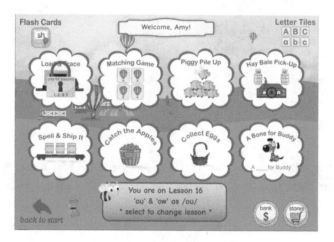

Copyright © 2014, 2015, 2018, 2020, 2021 All rights reserved.
Some Images used in this book are licensed and
copyrighted by © www.GraphicsFactory.com

Published By Blast Off to Learning Press
New York

e-mail all inquiries to
contact@BlastOffToLearningPress.com

Printed in the United States of America

I Can Fly Reading Program, Book B - Edition 1 - REV D
ISBN: 978-0-9831996-8-7

Table of Contents

Reading Program Notes

1. The **physical books** (books A & B) contains the *complete* reading program; there are no other components required. To augment the program, there are physical phonics games/tools and a web app available at our site. The web app and the physical games/tools are not part of the sale of this book. The web app is available as a free bonus add-on for those who have purchased the books, and may not work on all devices. In addition, at some future date, the web app may not be updated or may not be available. Please check our site to ensure that the app is still available.

2. For tutors and teachers who **instruct remotely**, there is a Kindle Teacher's Manual available. A Kindle device is not required since you can download Amazon's Kindle app to Macs and PCs. This manual contain instructions for the teacher, slides for presenting the lessons, and all lesson pages from this book. Visit www.BlastOffToLearningPress.com for more information.

How to use the Web App

1. Go to www.ICanFlyReadingProgram.com.

2. If using a tablet or phone, save the page to the home-screen and then re-open the app from the home-screen.

3. Select "Activate a Book" (on the left side).

4. Once you accept the Terms & Conditions, you will be taken to the activation page. Select the book you own (for this book it will be Book B - color interior).

5. You will then be asked to look in your book for a word to enter. Go to the page in the book and find the word and enter it. You will then have access to the web app. You can activate the app on more than one device if needed. *However, as stated in the Terms & Conditions, there can only be one user at a time per purchased book and sharing codes is not allowed.*

6. When you go back to the app's start-up page (the title page), you will see six slots, on the right side. Select a slot and enter your student's name. You can enter up to six students.

7. Next, select "Play" in the lower right corner. This will take you to the games. Some games are locked and will be unlocked when you select certain lessons. The lessons follow the sequence of this program.

8. The upper left corner contains the flash cards which you should review at the start of each lesson. The upper right corner contains letter tiles, which is a tool to review the sounds and rules that were taught.

9. Your student will collect coins and be able to make purchases as they play.

10. If using the web app, **be sure to periodically save the state of the app.** If your browser is cleared, all student names, metrics, coins, and scenes will be deleted. If this happens, if you saved the state, then you can restore it. Read the instructions on the title page (in the lower left) on how to save and restore the state of the web app.

11. To see your student's progress, go to the title page and select your student's name from "Accounts". Your student's metrics chart will be displayed.

Review
Flash Cards

Sometimes 'ow' has a long 'o' sound.

ow
as 'o'

ow = 'o'

Remember, 'ow' can **also** sound like /ou/.

ow = ou

crow	blow
bow	mow

b<u>ow</u> and arr<u>ow</u>

Trace the words below - remember to say the
sounds out loud as you write them.
When you write 'ow' you should say 'o'.

tow truck

pillow

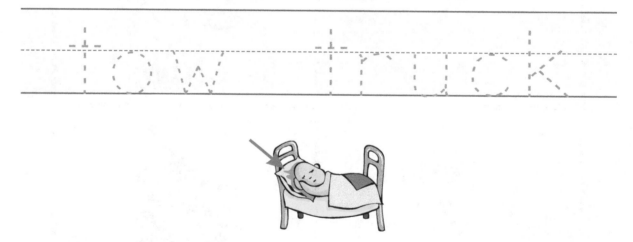

Draw lines to match the words with their pictures.

1. bow

2. arrow

3. blow

4. crow

5. pillow

6. mow

pillow, crow, arrow, bow, mow, blow

Circle the picture that goes with the sentence.

It will grow in the ground.

I know how to hit a ball.

Blow out the candles to make a wish!

The man will throw a ball.

Write the word that makes sense on the line.

Read the sentences to your student, but (s)he should read the answers in the box.

follow   grow   slow   flow

1. The opposite of fast is __?__ .

_____

- -

_____

2. Water will __?__ out of the faucet.

_____

- -

_____

3. The baby chicks will __?__ their mother.

_____

- -

_____

4. If you plant a seed, then it will __?__ .

_____

- -

_____

slow, flow, follow, grow

The frog only likes to eat words where 'ow'
has the long 'o' sound.
Circle the words where 'ow' is a long 'o' (there are 3).

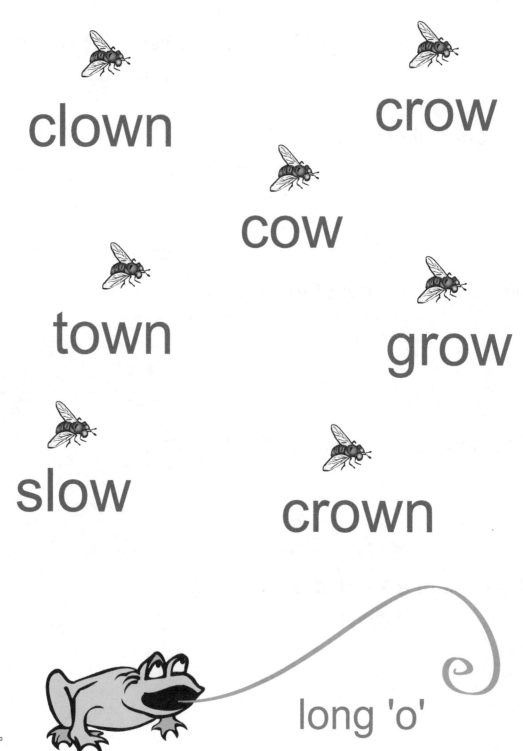

clown

crow

cow

town

grow

slow

crown

long 'o'

crow, grow, slow

VCV Review
Show the fairy which vowel needs the magic fairy dust
so that it can become a long vowel.
Circle the vowels that become long,
and read the words out loud.

spin - spine

shin - shine

tap - tape

tub - tube

pin - pine

kit - kite

Circle the picture that goes with the sentence.

1. I ate a stack of pancakes.

2. The clown is tossing the ball.

3. The fish is swimming in the bowl.

4. We went bowling and had fun!

5. My pillow is on my bed.

Draw lines to match the words with their pictures.

1. broom

2. crown

3. cloud

4. sock

5. cane

6. snow-flake

snow-flake, cane, broom, crown, sock, cloud

Draw lines to match the sentences to their pictures.

1. My pocket-book is in his mouth.

2. He will ride on her back.

3. The food is in the bag.

4. They made a snowman.

5. The scarecrow was outside.

Draw lines to match the words with their pictures.

1. spoon

2. pipe

3. pouch

4. spool

5. bowl

6. crack

spool, pipe, spoon, crack, bowl, pouch

Circle the picture that goes with the sentence.

1. He has a long neck.

2. The black crow sits on the branch.

3. He will wash his hands.

4. The dish is in the sink.

5. The chick is still small.

Complete the words below.

	ack	ank	ake

1.

c _____

	ell	ill	all

2.

b _____

	atch	ash	ath

3.

b _____

	ing	ink	ick

4.

w _____

	ock	otch	onk

5.

r _____

	ick	ike	ack

6.

b _____

cake, bell, bath, wink, rock, bike

Review

Read the words below.

slow	follow	how
grow	flow	now
snow	show	cow

shout	brown	mouse
town	clown	house

Read and trace the sentence, filling in the missing letters.

We m de a

sn man.

'ay' always has a long 'a' sound.

ay
as 'a'

ay = 'a'

w<u>ay</u>   pl<u>ay</u>

d<u>ay</u>   st<u>ay</u>

m<u>ay</u>   tr<u>ay</u>

I like to pl<u>ay</u> basketball.

Circle the picture that goes with the sentence.

1. The kitten will lay on the couch.

 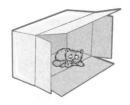 

2. My tooth may fall out today.

  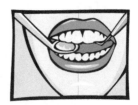

3. My lunch was on a tray.

4. I will write with a crayon.

Draw lines to match the words with their pictures.

1. pray

2. bowl

3. hay

4. plane

5. tray

6. mouth

hay, mouth, pray, tray, bowl, plane

Circle the picture that goes with the sentence.

The fish will stay in the bowl.

May I have a cupcake?

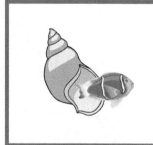  

She will lay on the sand.

He will pay the man with cash.

Circle the picture that goes with the sentence.

1. The cat will play
   with string.

2. The mouse hides
   in the hole.

3. Add a pinch of
   salt to the food.

4. He is black
   and white.

5. He will shout
   out loud.

Review:
Help the cowboy lasso up all of the pictures that
have the /ou/ sound as in "<u>ou</u>ch" and "<u>ow</u>l" (there are 5).

/ou/

cloud, mouth, cow, crown, clown

Review
Fill in the missing letters to compete the words.

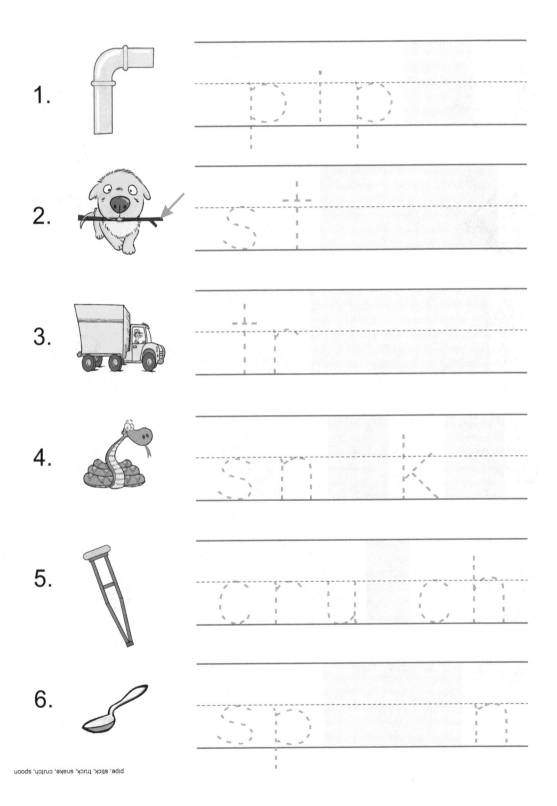

1. p i p _

2. s t _ _

3. _ t r _

4. s n _ k _

5. _ cru _ ch

6. sp _ _ n

pipe, stick, truck, snake, crutch, spoon

Draw lines to match the sounds to pictures that have the same sound.

1.    ing

2.   ock

3.    ay

4.    sh

5.   ench

6.   ick

tray, fish, sock, ring, chick, bench

Review

Read the words below.

they	drill	booth
stay	pill	tooth
tray	fill	spoon

blow	grow	show
blown	grown	shown

Read and trace the sentence, filling in the missing letters.

She will pl

a song.

A pirate says, "Arrrr!"
Now say the words to the pictures below
and see if you can hear the /ar/ sound.

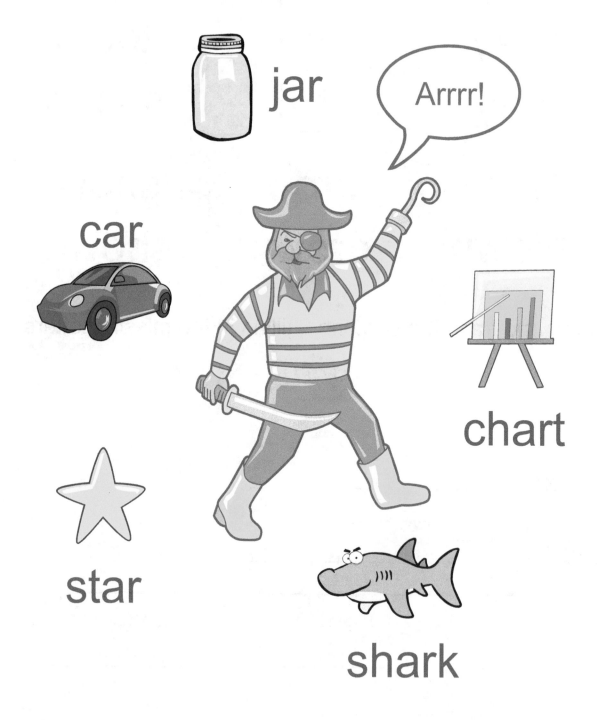

'ar' makes the /ar/ sound.

Trace the letters for the words for each picture, and **circle** the letters that make the /ar/ sound.
Remember to say the sounds as you write.

1.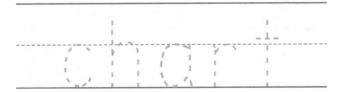

2.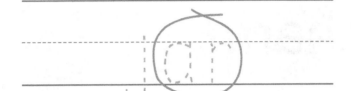

3.

4.

5.

Draw lines to match the words with their pictures.

1. jar

2. charm

3. star

4. arm

5. farm

6. car

star, arm, car, jar, charm, farm

Draw lines to match the words with their pictures.

1. art

2. shark

3. barn

4. yard

5. cart

6. dart

barn, dart, art, cart, shark, yard

Help the cowboy lasso up all of the pictures that have the /ar/ sound (there are 3).

 /ar/

jar, star, car

'or' makes the /or/ sound.
Many 'or' words end with a "do nothing" 'e'.

Trace the letters for the words for each picture,
and **circle** the letters that make the /or/ sound.
Remember to say the sounds as you write.

1. core

2. store

3. shore

4. snore

5. score

Read the sentences, and then choose the word in the box that completes the statement.

See how these 'or' words have a "do nothing" 'e' at the end ?

chore	more	sore	store

_____

1. I do not want less, I want _____ .

_____

2. We shop in a _____ .

_____

3. Making my bed is a _____ .

_____

4. If I run too much my legs get _____ .

more, store, chore, sore

A few /or/ words have an extra 'o'

d<u>oo</u>r   fl<u>oo</u>r   p<u>oo</u>r

There are no "do nothing 'e's" in these words.

Circle the picture that goes with the sentence.

1. The door is
    open.

2. She will wash
    the floor.

3. The man was
    poor.

'ir' and 'ur' have the **same** sound as 'er'.

st<u>ir</u>   b<u>ur</u>n   fast<u>er</u>

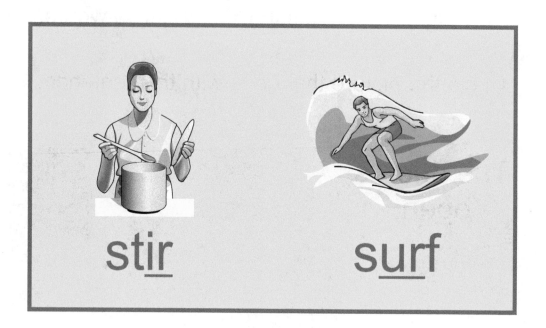

Review flash cards before
each lesson.

Either make your own, or use
the online app that goes with
this program.

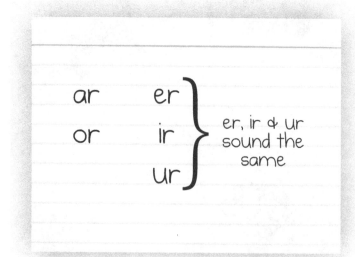

'er' is *usually* at the end of a word.

fast<u>er</u>   small<u>er</u>

Read the sentence and circle the word that makes sense.

1. The rabbit runs <u>shorter / faster</u> than me.

2. My hamster is <u>longer / smaller</u> than my cat.

3. At the end of the day it gets <u>darker / slower</u>.

faster, smaller, darker

are = ar

were = w + er

The last 'e', in both words,
does nothing at all!

Remember Bleep? He's back and wants to learn more words from our language.
Circle the words that make sense.

Read the sentence to your student, but do not read the answer choices.

1. The opposite of long is _____.

short   sport   far

2. The opposite of near is _____.

form   far   curb

3. Our birthday is the day that we were _____.

born   torn   first

4. This is another name for woods _____.

fort   forest   part

short, far, born, forest

Circle the picture that goes with the sentence.

1. The man is a foot-ball player.

2. We were playing card games.

  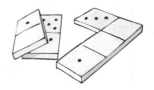

3. We are having cake on my birthday.

4. How hard is it to jump ten times?

Circle the picture that goes with the sentence.

The girl is smart.

Stir the pot with the spoon.

Do not burn your arm on the stove top.

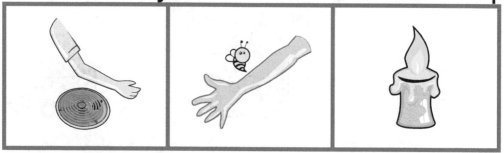

We put the food in our shopping cart.

Circle the pictures that go with the sentences.

1. We had to call a tow truck for our car.

2. We were going down to the shore.

3. We are going to the store to stock up on food.

4. The book was about a poor man.

5. The fire cracker makes a loud sound.

Read the sentences and circle the words that make sense.

1. The boy likes to <u>surf / fall</u>.

2. The cowgirl can <u>play / snore</u>.

3. The <u>fingers / sisters</u> are together.

4. We will serve corn for <u>dinner / diner.</u>

5. My father has to <u>woke / work</u> late.

work = /w<u>er</u>k/

Circle the **sound** that is in the word for each picture.

1.   ow   or   ay

2.    ay   er   ou

3.   ow   oo   ay

4.    er   ar   or

5.    er   ay   or

6.   ar   oo   ay

corn, tray, broom, jar, door, star

Draw lines to match the words with their pictures.

1. flower

2. shower

3. mower

4. power

5. boxer

6. timer

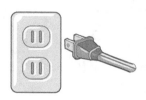

Review

Read the words below.

car	dirt	floor
cart	skirt	door
part	stir	poor

more	shower	banker
store	power	sticker
chore	player	rocker

Trace the words for the pictures filling in the missing letters.

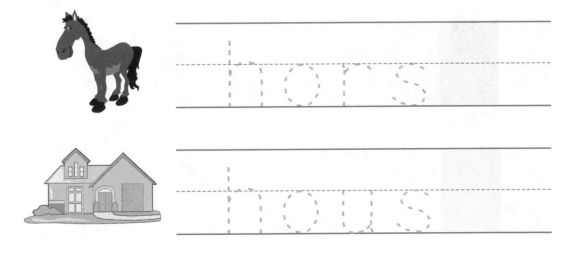

hors

hous

Review flash cards
every day!

oy
oi

There are **two** ways to get the
/oy/ sound as in "boy".

oy   oi

b<u>oy</u>

b<u>oi</u>l

t<u>oy</u>

c<u>oi</u>l

Underline the /oy/ sound and read the words out loud.

joy   foil

toy   coil

boy   broil

* Notice how 'oy' is usually at the <u>end</u> of a word,
and 'oi' is usually in the <u>middle</u> of a word.

Trace the word for each picture and **circle** the /oy/ sound.

1.  coin

2. 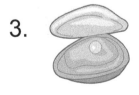 point

3. 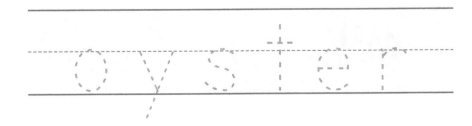 oyster

Draw lines to match the words with their pictures.

1. boy

2. toy

3. chart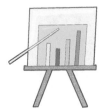

4. coil

5. point

6. jar

point, chart, boy, jar, coil, toy

Read the passage below.

To make a moist cake, add oil.
You may need to add an egg too.
Do not forget the milk!
Mix it all up.
Put it in the oven.
The house will smell good!
Take it out.
Let the cake cool.
Put frosting on top.
Yum yum!
Time to have some cake!

One picture below does NOT have anything to do with the passage above. Cross that picture out.

Circle the pictures that go with the sentences.

1. A plant will grow well in moist soil.

2. I will wrap my lunch in tin-foil.

3. I put a coin into my pocketbook.

4. I will join grandpa on a fishing trip.

Circle the **sound** that is in the word for each picture.

1.   oi   or   ay

2.    oo   oy   ou

3.    unk   ock   uck

4.    ay   ou   oi

5.    er   ar   or

6.   ing   ink   ick

coil, pool, truck, house, shark, ring

Review
Draw lines to match the words with their pictures.

1. pray

2. shark

3. switch

4. sing

5. barn

6. plane

plane, sing, barn, pray, shark, switch

Review
Draw lines to match the words with their pictures.

* Remember, words with 'or' often have a "do nothing" 'e' at the end *

1. core

2. shore

3. door

4. score

5. snore

6. store

shore, store, core, snore, score, door

Choose the words that go with the sentences, and
write them on the lines.

car	joy	floor	star

1. The boy will
   jump for ___.

   _____

2. We will ride
   in the ___.

   _____

3. Make a wish
   on a shooting ___.

   _____

4. My dog got mud
   all over the ___.

   _____

joy, car, star, floor

Circle the pictures that make sense for the sentences below.

1. The boy took a nap in his bed.

2. He points with his finger.

3. Put the food in the trunk of the car.

4. Why are you at the store?

5. The gray cat likes to chase birds.

Review

Help the cowboy lasso up all of the words that
have the /ou/ sound as in "<u>ou</u>t" and "<u>ow</u>l" (there are 5).

cow

crown

owl

grow

town

sound

own

cow, owl, crown, town, sound

Choose the sounds to finish the words below.

	it	ite	ick

1. k_____

	ank	ack	ake

2. sn_____

	or	ar	er

3. st_____

	ou	ow	or

4. h_____se

	ir	ar	or

5. h_____p

	ou	ow	oi

6. c_____n

Draw lines from the words to their matching pictures.

1. racket

2. coin

3. purse

4. tape

5. shower

6. rake

coin, purse, racket, shower, rake, tape

Review

Read the words below.

| joy | soil | tinfoil |
| toy | spoil | pointer |

| hard | dark | start |
| harder | darker | starter |

Read and trace the sentence, filling in the missing letters.

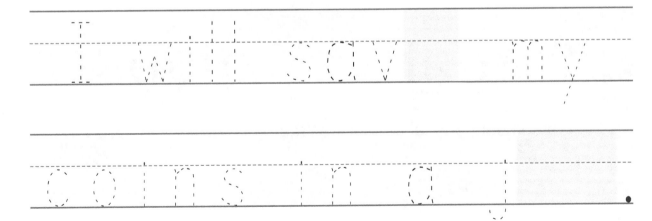

I will sav my

coins in a j.

We can get a **long** vowel sound two ways.
1) When a vowel is one hop away, as in the word "kite".
2) When **two** vowels are **next** to each other.

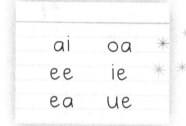

ai	oa
ee	ie
ea	ue

There's that fairy again, sprinkling magic fairy dust on nearby vowels, making them long!

p<u>ai</u>l   b<u>oa</u>t

t<u>ee</u>th   p<u>ie</u>

r<u>ea</u>l   gl<u>ue</u>

Remember: long 'u' *usually* has the /oo/ sound as in "boo".

ū   Boo!

Below are the common vowel teams that are usually used. The first vowel says its name, and the second vowel is *usually* silent.

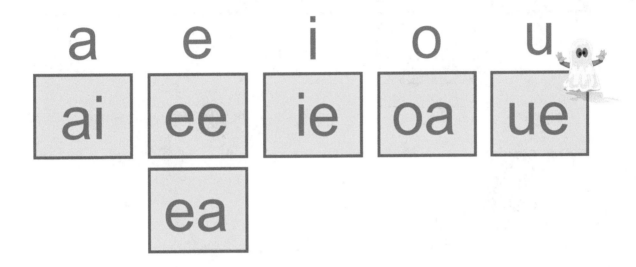

a e i o u

| ai | ee | ie | oa | ue |

| ea |

Trace the vowel teams below.

a ai   i ie

e ee   o oa

e ea   u ue

Choose the vowel teams to compete the words.

ai	ee	ie	oa	ue

ea

1.  t _ _ l

2.  g _ _ t

3. 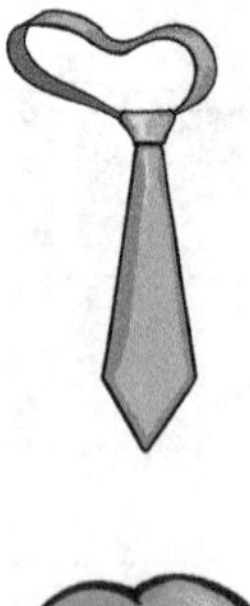 t _ _

4.  p _ _ ch

tail, goat, tie, peach

Draw lines to match the words to their colors.

1. blue

2. green

3. yellow

4. purple

5. pink

6. red

7. brown

Draw lines from the words to their matching pictures.

1. pail

2. pie

3. sail

4. train

5. boat

6. tree

tree, train, pail, pie, sail, boat

Draw lines from the words to their pictures.

barn   cloud   rake   farmer

horse   cow   pail

pitchfork   tree

Circle the picture that goes with the sentence.

1. A spider can make a web.

2. A palm tree can grow a coconut.

3. My mother likes to drink tea.

4. The boy will read the book.

Label the compass with the correct directions.

If your student does not know what a compass is, explain it to him/her.
To help remember the names, you can use the sentence
"Never eat soggy waffles" going clockwise.

| north | west | south | east |

_____

_____

_____   **N**   _____
--------------------------------   --------------------------------
_____   **W** —◆— **E**   _____

S

_____

_____

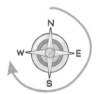

<u>N</u>ever <u>e</u>at <u>s</u>oggy <u>w</u>affles.

Bleep is back and wants to learn more words from our language. Circle the words that make sense.

Encourage your student to read BOTH the clues and the answers, help out if needed.

1. The opposite of fake is ___.

good   real   feel

2. We do this with our lungs ___.

breathe   snore   eat

3. This falls from the clouds ___.

birds   rain   beans

4. When we sleep we can have a ___.

feet   moon   dream

real, breathe, rain, dream

Label the pictures by drawing lines from the words to the part of the picture that the word belongs to.

beak   wing   tail

ear   chin   mouth   cheek

Review
Draw lines to match the words with their pictures.

1. soap

2. tape

3. bake

4. boil

5. chase

6. smoke

tape, chase, boil, soap, smoke, bake

Read the sentence and then circle the word that makes sense.

1. Use <u>food / soap</u> to wash your hands.

2. I want to <u>feed / keep</u> that shirt.

3. I <u>sleep / swim</u> in my bed.

4. It is his job to <u>feed / eat</u> the dog.

5. We will <u>hide / meet</u> you at five o'clock.

6. The <u>deer / shark</u> ran into the woods.

soap, keep, sleep, feed, meet, deer

Circle the picture that goes with the sentence.

1. The girl went to the beach.

2. The dentist will look at my teeth.

3. The ball hit his knee.

4. The rain came down hard.

5. My house is down the street.

Review

Read the words below.

tree	meal	goat
three	speak	boat
see	bean	f^loat

bite	name	side
hide	same	kite
wide	game	like

Complete the words below.

  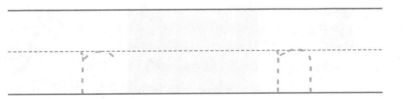

3

In the beginnning of a word, 'y' has the consonant sound for 'y' as in the word "yellow".

At the end of a word, 'y' acts like a vowel and can sound like a long 'e' or a long 'i'.

> At the end of a word
> 'y' can sound like
> a long 'i' or a long 'e'

cry

'y' sounds like long

_____

_____

happy

'y' sounds like long

_____

_____

Read the words to your student, and have him/her write
the sound (long 'i' or long 'e') that the 'y' or 'ey' makes.

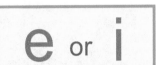

spy

key

fly

baby

monkey

cry

itchy

pony

Not only does 'y' **sound** like a vowel, it also **acts** like a vowel. It can turn another vowel **long** if it is close enough.

baby

key

Circle the **vowel** that the 'y' makes **long.**

p<u>o</u>n<u>y</u>

monk<u>e</u>y

mon<u>e</u>y

l<u>a</u>d<u>y</u>

pony, money, monkey, lady

Circle the basket that has the same sound as the 'y'
in the word in the apple.

1.

long 'e' long 'i'

2.  long 'e' long 'i'

3.   long 'e' long 'i'

4.   long 'e' long 'i'

5.   long 'e' long 'i'

1) long 'i', 2) long 'e', 3) long 'e', 4) long 'i', 5) long 'e'

Circle the picture that goes with the sentence.

The baby cried loudly.

The lady is a teacher.

The dirty boy takes a bath.

The hungry girl ate lunch.

The frog only likes to eat words where the 'y' has the long 'i' sound. Circle the words where **'y' is a long 'i'** (hint: there are 4).

tiny

my

cry

funny

try

fly

windy

long 'i'

Review
Trace the vowel teams below.

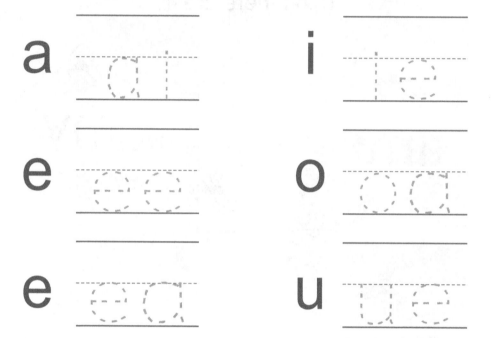

a

e

e

i

o

u

Fill in the vowel teams.

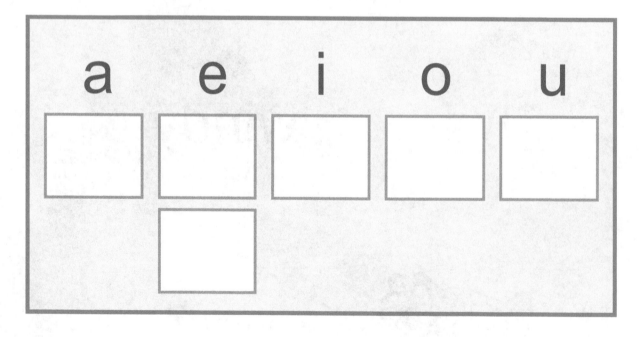

a   e   i   o   u

Review
Draw lines to match the words to their pictures.

1. sting

2. sleep

3. chart

4. mermaid

5. train

6. soap

mermaid, chart, soap, sleep, sting, train

Bleep is back and wants to learn more words from our language. Circle the words that make sense.

Encourage your student to read both the clues and the answers.

1. Something that is very small is ___.

tiny   spiny   runny

2. We laugh when something is ___.

money   nasty   funny

3. When bitten by a bug, our skin may get ___.

itchy   silly   spiny

4. When the wind blows, we say that it is ___.

cozy   jolly   windy

tiny, funny, itchy, windy

Review
Draw lines to match the words to their pictures.

1. pie

2. tie

3. teeth

4. tape

5. glue

6. peach

teeth, tape, pie, glue, peach, tie

Read the sentence and then circle the word that makes sense.

1. Hide and seek is a story / game.

2. In the winter it may snow / sleep.

3. They plant flowers in the soil / food.

4. She said a funny / hungry joke.

5. On Sunday, we went to the lamp / party.

6. On Monday, it will be rusty / cloudy.

game, snow, soil, funny, party, cloudy

Circle the picture that goes with the sentence.

1. She will try to catch the ball.

2. The baby will cry for his mother.

3. The fire was warm and cozy.

4. The boy ate too many jelly beans.

5. The man will fry the fish for dinner.

Fill in the missing letters for the words.

ai oi ow eck ee ou

1. b☐☐

2.  n☐☐☐

3. h☐☐se

4.  s☐☐l

5.  tr☐☐

6. p☐☐nt

bow, neck, house, sail, tree, point

Review

Read the words below.

sleep - sleepy   slow - slowly

rock - rocky   bad - badly

sun - sunny   quick - quickly

Read and trace the sentence, filling in the missing letters.

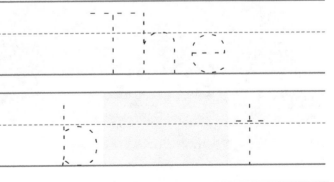

the

b t

is on the lak .

Review flash cards.

Just like 'y' can sound like a long 'e' at the end of a word, 'ie' can also sound like a long 'e' at the end of a word.

At the end of a word

'ie' sounds like

long 'e'

 cookie

doggie

 genie

 brownie

★ Words that end with **just** an 'e' do NOT make the long 'e' sound. ★

Draw lines to match the words to their pictures.

1. ## hoodie

2. ## bootie

3. ## movie

4. ## birdie

5. ## brownie

6. ## cookie

bootie, movie, brownie, hoodie, cookie, birdie

Many times a word is not spelled the way it sounds.

Sound the word out, and then, if it is not a word that you know, see if you can change the word a little bit, so it becomes a word you do know.

movie sounds like **m<u>oo</u>vie**

money sounds like **munny**

what sounds like **wut**

some sounds like **sum**

sure sounds like **shur**

?

Circle the picture that goes with the sentence.

The baby is a cutie.

I want to see a movie.

The genie gave me three wishes.

The baby wore pink booties.

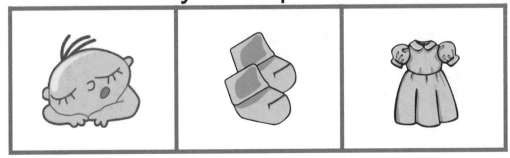

Review
Fill in the vowel teams.

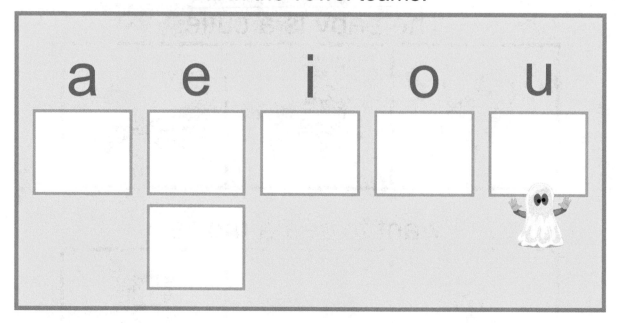

a   e   i   o   u

Circle the vowel teams and read the words out loud.

green   pie

pain   teeth

float   nail

The frog only likes to eat words where
'ie' has the **long 'e' sound**.
Circle the **three** words where 'ie' makes the
long 'e' sound.

cookie

birdie

pie

tie

doggie

long 'e'

cookie, birdie, doggie

We can add 'ing' to many words.
Circle the picture that goes with the sentence.

1. The man is box<u>ing</u>.

2. The man is sing<u>ing</u>.

3. The boy is sleep<u>ing</u>.

4. The lady is teach<u>ing</u>.

5. The boy is digg<u>ing</u>.

6. The fish is swimm<u>ing</u>.

Review
Circle the picture that matches the word.

1. couch

2. maid

3. owl

4. pumpkin

5. towel

6. toad

Choose the sounds to finish the words below.

1.  | or | er | ar |

2.  | ee | oa | ai |

3. 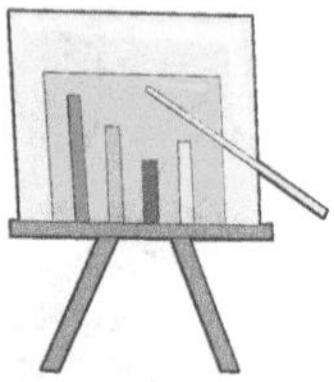 | ar | or | ir |

4.  | oa | ea | ie |

5.  | oa | ue | ou |

6.  | er | or | ar |

Review

Read the words below.

cookie	funny	tooth
brownie	sleepy	teeth
goodie	sunny	mouth

paint - painting

jump - jumping

wait - waiting

Fill in the letters to spell the words for the pictures.

_____ _____ _____

_____ _____ _____

* Be careful, this word has an 'a' that sounds like a short 'o'.

_____ _____ _____ _____ _____

_____ _____ _____ _____ _____

owl, watch

'ew' *usually* sounds like /oo/, as in "boo", but sometimes it sounds like 'u'.

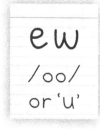

ew
/oo/
or 'u'

oo!

Or 'u'!

* 'ew' usually sounds like /oo/ *

The bird **fl<u>ew</u>** away.

The volcano will **sp<u>ew</u>** lava.

Read the sentence and circle the word that makes sense.

1. The sunflower <u>grow / grew</u> tall.

2. The wind <u>blew / blue</u> hard.

3. I have a <u>few / flew</u> coins in my pocket.

4. He <u>brew / drew</u> with a marker.

5. The ship had a <u>crew / crow</u> of ten men.

6. The cow will <u>chew / grow</u> the grass.

grew, blew, few, drew, crew

Circle the picture that goes with the sentence.

We will cook the stew over a fire.

The car was brand new.

The boy blew out the candles.

The bird flew away.

Review
Fill in the vowel teams.

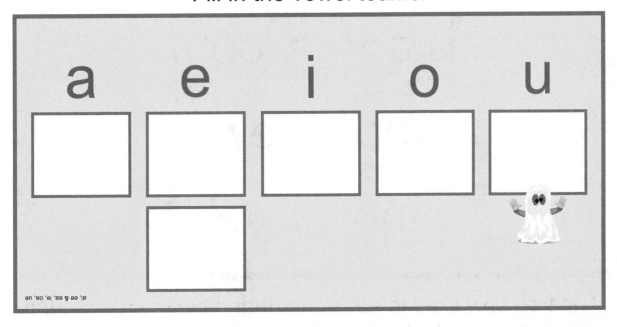

a   e   i   o   u

ai, ee & ea, ie, oa, ue

Circle the vowel teams and read the words out loud.

train   week

knee   road

read   true

There are **three** ways to get the /oo/, as in "boo", sound.

$$/oo/ = 'oo'$$

$$/oo/ = 'ew'$$

$$/oo/ = 'ue'$$

The frog only likes to eat words that have the /oo/ sound.
Circle the words that have the /oo/ sound (there are 2).

flew   few   true

flew, true

We can add 'ing' to many words.
Circle the picture that goes with the sentence.

1. The man is runn<u>ing</u>.

2. The cow is chew<u>ing</u>.

3. The baby is drink<u>ing</u>.

4. The boy is cry<u>ing</u>.

5. The fish is fry<u>ing</u>.

6. The cook is stirr<u>ing</u>.

The 'ew' in the words below all have the /oo/ sound **except** for one. Read the words out loud and see if you can find the one that has the long 'u' sound.

new	stew
grew	flew
knew	brew
chew	few
drew	
crew	

* 'ew' as 'u' is not very popular.

Review
Circle the picture that goes with the word.

1. cookie

2. knee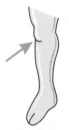

3. yell

4. farmer

5. washing

6. horse

Review
Fill in the missing letters for the words.

1. g ☐ ☐ t

2. p ☐ ☐

3. p ☐ ☐ l

4. c ☐ ☐ n

5. p ☐ ☐ l

6. c ☐ ☐ ☐

Review
Draw lines to match the words to their pictures.

1. sky

2. soap

3. hand

4. hook

5. scrub

6. key

Review

Read the words below.

crew   stew

new   drew

grow - grew

fly - flew

blow - blew

jelly   smelly   stinky

Write the words for the pictures on the lines below.

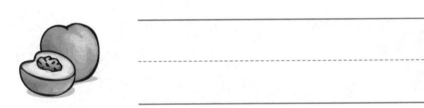

peach, boat

old
ind

Sometimes we get a long vowel
sound for no reason at all.

The 'o' in 'old' makes a **long 'o' sound**,
and the 'i' in 'ind' *usually* make the **long 'i' sound.**

g<u>o</u>ld	f<u>i</u>nd
s<u>o</u>ld	m<u>i</u>nd
f<u>o</u>ld	gr<u>i</u>nd
c<u>o</u>ld	k<u>i</u>nd

Some words can be pronounced two different ways:

wind   wind

Draw lines to match the words to their pictures.

1. cold

2. fold

3. hold

4. old

5. folder

6. gold

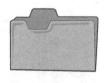

old, gold, fold, hold, cold, folder

Circle the picture that goes with the sentence.

He will fold the paper.

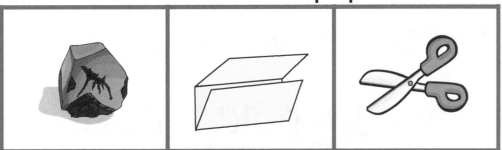

We sold our house.

Grandma will hold the baby.

We found the pot of gold.

Bleep is back and wants to learn more words from our language. Circle the words that make sense.

Encourage your student to read the questions (as well as the answers).

1. We think with our ___.

   mind   bold   nose

2. If you are very nice, you are ___.

   fold   kind   old

3. If something is not old, it may be ___.

   small   sold   new

4. If we look for something we may ___ it.

   find   fond   fund

mind, kind, new, find

Circle the picture that goes with the sentence.

1. You put this on when it is cold out.

2. For my birthday, I got a new kite.

3. The lady pushes the old woman.

4. This goes around your neck when it is cold.

5. The teacher told him to get the book.

6. My father sold his old car.

Draw lines to match the words to their pictures.

1. **blindfold**

2. **blind**

3. **wind**

4. **binder**

5. **grinder**

6. **mind**

binder, wind, grinder, blindfold, mind, blind

Below are some special words that
have their own long 'i' sounds.

wild
child
mild

w<u>i</u>ld

ch<u>i</u>ld

m<u>i</u>ld

To remember these three words, ask your mother
if you are a wild child or a mild child.

Circle which type of baby you were.

mild child   wild child

Review
Fill in the vowel teams.

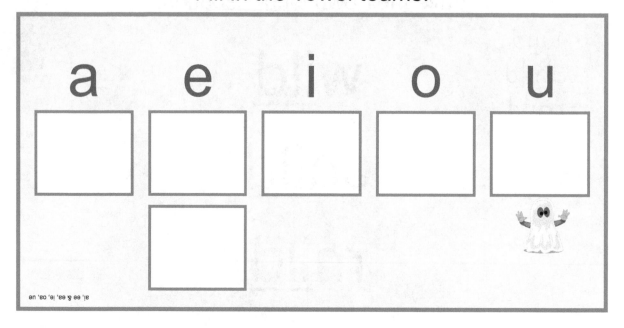

Circle the vowel teams and read the words out loud.

feel   plain

real   true

need   please

The frog only likes to eat words that have the long 'i' sound.
Circle the words that have the long 'i' sound (there are 4).

kind

children

find

windmill

wilt

wild

child

long 'i'

kind, find, wild, child

Review
Circle the picture that matches the word.

1. scarf

2. toy

3. jacket

4. bowl

5. burger

6. mouse

We can add 'ing' to many words.
Circle the picture that goes with the sentence.

1. The boy is read**ing**.

2. The wind is blow**ing**.

3. The old lady was cook**ing**.

4. The boy is surf**ing**.

5. The milk is spill**ing**.

6. The man was drill**ing**.

Below are some special words that have their own long 'o' sounds.

most	roll
host	scroll
post	troll
ghost	toll

m<u>o</u>st   r<u>o</u>ll

h<u>o</u>st   scr<u>o</u>ll

p<u>o</u>st   tr<u>o</u>ll

gh<u>o</u>st   t<u>o</u>ll

Remember: 'ow' and 'oa' can also sound like a long 'o'.

 cr<u>ow</u>    gh<u>o</u>st

 b<u>oa</u>t    r<u>o</u>ll

That's four ways to get a long 'o' sound!

Draw lines to match the words to their pictures.

1. post

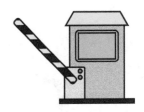

2. troll

3. scroll

4. roll

5. toll

6. ghost

ghost, roll, toll, post, scroll, troll

The first sound for each word is above the picture.
Circle the letters that finish the word.

1.

scr

ole

oal

oll

2.

r

ind

old

oll

3.

h

old

oll

ole

4.

f

old

oll

ind

5.

w

ent

ind

end

6.

h

ouse

orse

ors

scroll, roll, hold, fold, wind, horse

Trace the letters and fill in the missing sounds.
Remember to say the sounds as you write them.

1.  b _ _ _ t

2.  c r _ _ _ _

3. 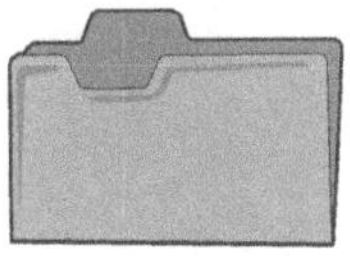 f _ _ _ _ _ e r

4.  b _ _ _ l

5.  g _ _ _ _

6. 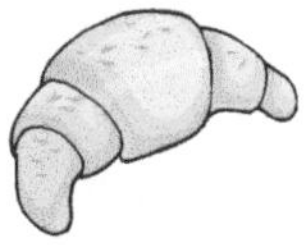 r _ _ _ _

bc̶ɑt, crow, folder, bowl, gold, roll

Read the sentence, choose the word that makes sense,
and write it on the line.

| blind | most | toll | old |

1. He has the least games, but I have the

_____

2. My grandfather is

_____

3. On a road trip you may have to pay a

_____

4. A person, who cannot see, may be

_____

most, old, toll, blind

Don't forget the periods!

Review
Draw lines to match the words to their pictures.

1. toilet

2. grinder

3. boot

4. sky

5. scarf

6. rainbow

sky, scarf, grinder, toilet, rainbow, boot

Review
Fill in the missing letters for the words.

1. n ☐ ☐ ☐

2. br ☐ ☐ ☐

3. ch ☐ ☐ ☐

4. br ☐ ☐ ☐

5. p ☐ ☐ ☐ ☐

6. m ☐ ☐ ☐

nail, brain, chain, braid, paint, maid

Review

Read the words below.

main	tail	grain
pain	rain	plain
stain	paid	wait

grow	child	roll
blow	children	most
show	wild	cold

Write the words, for the pictures, on the lines below.
Remember, say the sounds as you write them,
do not say the letter names.

scarf, bank

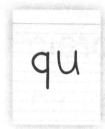

'q' and 'u' are **best friends** and are *always* next to each other.
Together, they make the /qu/ sound as in "queen".

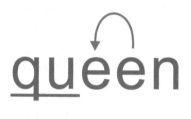

queen

quilt

quiet

In the word "quiet", you also hear the 'e' for /et/.

Draw lines to match the words to their pictures.

1. square

2. squirrel

3. equal

4. quotes

5. squid

6. squirt

quotes, squid, square, squirrel, squirt, equals

Sometimes 'q' has a tail.	And sometimes 'q' does **not** have a tail.
q	q

Read the sentences and complete the words.

1. A duck likes to ___.

_ _ _ _ c k

2. A shape with 4 equal sides is a ___.

s _ _ _ a r e

3. A quick test is a ___.

_ _ _ _ i z

Bleep is back and wants to learn more words from our language. Circle the words that make sense.

Encourage your student to read the questions (as well as the answers).

1. The opposite of loud is ___.

   quiet   quit   quite

2. A type of a blanket is a ___.

   quit   quite   quilt

3. Another word for "fast" is ___.

   quick   quiet   quest

4. If you want to stop doing something you may ___.

   quest   quite   quit

quiet, quilt, quick, quit

Circle the picture that goes with the sentence.

This shape is a square.

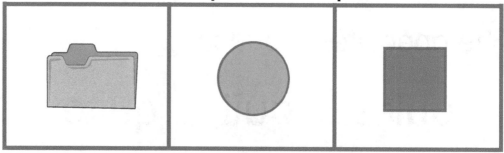

The man will do ten squats.

The pig will squeal loud.

You must be quiet.

Review
Circle the picture that goes with the sentence.

1. He may scare you.

2. The key may open the door.

3. This can roll down a hill.

4. Every hive has a queen bee.

5. It was very windy outside on the beach.

6. The quick cat can catch the mouse.

Draw lines to match the words to their pictures.

1. quiet

2. cry

3. queen

4. pinch

5. quilt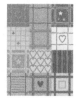

6. cookie

queen, cookie, pinch, quilt, quiet, cry

Review
Unscramble the words to make a sentence.
Remember: the first letter in the first word gets
capitalized, and don't forget the period.

scare   ghost
                        a
you   can

1) _____

- -

_____

_____

- -

_____

A ghost can scare you.

hats

lady

likes

red   the

2) _____

- -

_____

_____

- -

_____

The lady likes red hats.

Review

Trace the letters and fill in the missing sounds.
Remember to say the sounds as you write them.

1.

t _ l e t

2.

c _ k i n g

3.

s c _ f

4.

c _ t

5.

t _

6.

m _ th

toilet, cooking, scarf, cart, toy, mouth

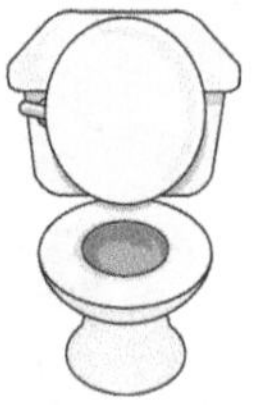

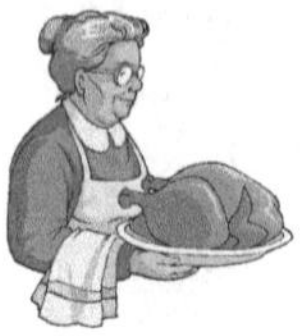

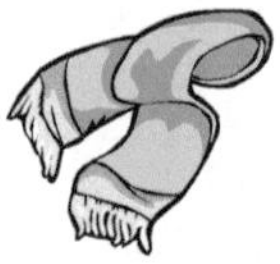

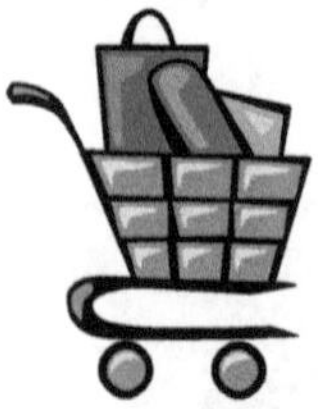

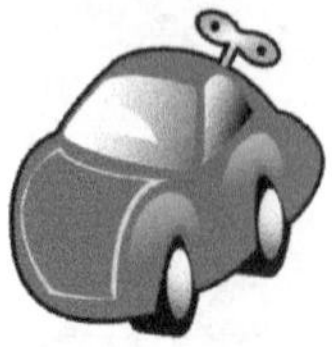

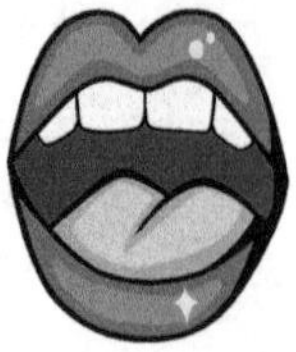

Review
Choose two pictures, and write a sentence for each.

1) _____

2) _____

Choose the sounds to finish the words below.

	ow	ou	oa
1.	c		d

	ai	ou	oa
2.	t	s	t

	ay	ar	ai
3.	t r		

	ar	oll	old
4.	f	e r	

	oa	ue	ou
5.	f	m	

	oa	ow	ou
6.	m	s e	

Review

Read the words below.

quit   square   far

quite   squirm   farther

quiet   squirt   father

tall   roll   jacket

call   bowl   pocket

ball   snow   racket

Write the words on the lines.

quilt, queen

Review flash cards
every day!

au
aw

Both 'au' and 'aw' have the
/aw/ sound as in "paw".

au   aw

p<u>aw</u>

Santa Cl<u>au</u>s

cr<u>aw</u>l

p<u>au</u>se

Words that end with 'a', end with the /uh/ sound
as in the word "Santa".

Draw lines to match the words to their pictures.

1. ## yawn

2. ## saw

3. ## hawk

4. ## claw

5. ## straw

6. ## draw

hawk, draw, straw, claw, yawn, saw

Circle the picture that goes with the sentence.

1. On Saturday morning, he mows the lawn.

2. After I wake up, I sometimes yawn.

3. The baby likes to draw.

4. The man will use a saw to cut the wood.

5. His claw can pinch your toe.

S 's' as the /z/ sound Z

Sometimes, words that end with an 'se' will end with the /z/ sound. We see this in the following words.

pau<u>se</u>

becau<u>se</u>

Match the words to their pictues.

1. ho<u>se</u>

2. ro<u>se</u>

3. toe<u>s</u>

4. no<u>se</u>

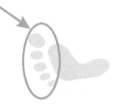

Bleep is back and wants to learn more words from our language. Circle the words that make sense.

Encourage your student to read the questions (as well as the answers).

1. When clothes are dirty you must do the ___.

laundry   because

2. If you are a girl, then you are a ___.

daughter   caught

3. A person who writes a book is an ___.

author   daughter

4. When we want to stop a song we press ___.

cause   pause

laundry, daughter, author, pause

Circle the correct word.

Part of your face is your ___.

jaw   paw   claw

I drink with a ___.

draw   claw   straw

If food is not cooked it is ___.

raw   yawn   saw

Food that is frozen will need to ___.

yawn   draw   thaw

To stay out of jail, you follow the ___.

law   flaw   saw

jaw, straw, raw, thaw, law

alk
/awk/

'alk' has the /awk/ sound **and is only in a few words** which are listed below.

w<u>al</u>k

t<u>al</u>k

st<u>al</u>k

b<u>al</u>k

ch<u>al</u>k

We can add 'ing' to many words.
Circle the picture that goes with the sentence.

1. The girl is talk<u>ing</u>.

2. The man is walk<u>ing</u>.

3. The boy is yawn<u>ing</u>.

4. The man is squirt<u>ing</u>.

5. The bee sting is hurt<u>ing</u>.

6. The boy is draw<u>ing</u>.

Review
Unscramble the words to make a sentence.
Remember: the first letter in the first word gets capitalized, and don't forget the period.

peach   I   will

a   eat   snack   for

1) _____

_____

_____

I will eat a peach for snack. OR For snack I will eat a peach.

grandma   my

for   dinner

turkey   made

2) _____

_____

_____

My grandma made turkey for dinner. Or: For dinner my grandma made turkey.

Draw lines to match the words to their pictures.

1. roll

2. quotes

3. rain

4. squirrel

5. quiet

6. maid

squirrel, rain, quiet, maid, roll, quotes

Read each sentence and circle the word that makes sense.

1. There are seven days in a <u>sleep / week</u>.

2. The back of my foot is my <u>heel / toe</u>.

3. Candy is very <u>sour / sweet</u>.

4. The number that is after two is <u>tree / three</u>.

5. I swim to the <u>deep / small</u> side of the pool.

6. Where do you <u>sleep / keep</u> your toys?

week, heel, sweet, three, deep, keep

Review
Choose two pictures, and write a sentence for each.

1)

_____

- -

_____

- -

_____

2)

_____

- -

_____

- -

_____

Read each sentence and circle the word that makes sense.

1. The old man was <u>grumpy / sticky</u>.

2. The skunk was <u>stinky / happy</u>.

3. The boots were <u>dirty / noisy</u>.

4. The road was <u>cheesy / bumpy</u>.

5. The baby was <u>sleepy / floppy</u>.

6. The old car was <u>chewy / rusty.</u>

grumpy, stinky, dirty, bumpy, sleepy, rusty

Review

Read the words below.

paw	talk	cause
draw	walk	because
crawl	chalk	noise

quit	holding	mess
quite	yawning	miss
quiet	bowling	less

Complete the word below.

dr

The 'ct' Sound

Review the flash cards.

You have to listen close for this 'ct' sound,
since it comes quick!

 <u>ac</u>tor

 ins<u>ec</u>t

 d<u>oc</u>tor

 str<u>ic</u>t

---

Read the sounds below to your student, and then have him/her read them back.
Note that all vowels are **short.**

act   ect   ict   oct   uct

act   oct

ect   uct

ict   All vowels
          are short.

Words with 'ct' are usually longer words.

inspector
in sp ect or

The <u>inspector</u> is looking for clues.

tractor
tr act or

The farmer rides on his <u>tractor</u>.

<u>O</u>ctober
Oct o ber

Halloween is at the end of <u>October</u>.

Draw lines to match the pictures to their words.

1. <u>oct</u>opus

2. subtr<u>act</u>

3. el<u>ect</u>ric

4. insp<u>ect</u>or

5. cond<u>uct</u>or

6. tr<u>act</u>or

electric, inspector, conductor, octopus, tractor, subtract

Review
Draw lines to match the pictures to their words.

1. straw

2. saw

3. point

4. draw

5. arrow

6. yawn

point, yawn, straw, arrow, draw, saw

Draw lines to match the sentences to their pictures.

1. His answer
was corr**ect**.

2. The boy will
coll**ect** toy cars.

3. What is the
ex**act** time?

4. The teacher
was str**ict**.

5. He will dir**ect**
the **act**or.

Circle the picture that goes with the sentence.

1. She is exp<u>ect</u>ing a new baby.

2. He will coll<u>ect</u> the trash.

3. It gets cold in <u>Oct</u>ober.

4. An ins<u>ect</u> landed on my hand.

5. If you are sick you may see a <u>doct</u>or.

Read the clue, then choose the word. You will have
to change the word so that it makes sense.
Write the new words on the lines.

ing

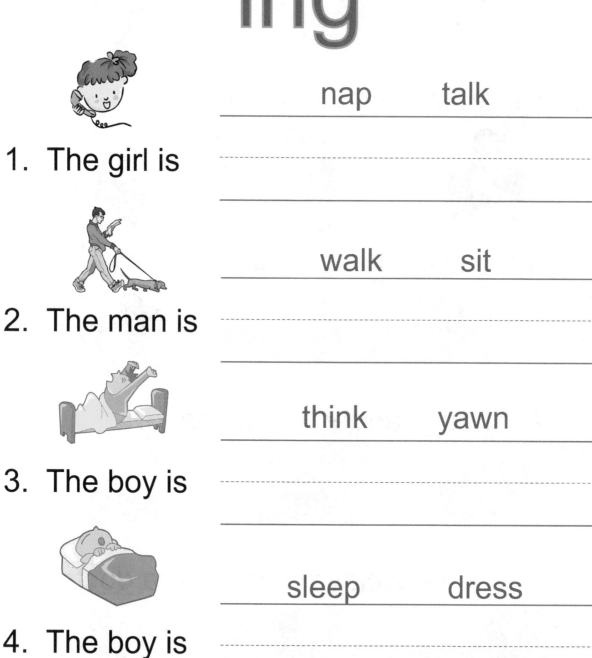

nap   talk

1. The girl is

walk   sit

2. The man is

think   yawn

3. The boy is

sleep   dress

4. The boy is

talking, walking, yawning, sleeping

Circle the correct word.

1. Something that is true is a ___.

   act   stack   fact

2. We make ___ when we cry.

   tears   pacts   paws

3. We ___ with our mouths.

   look   walk   talk

4. A doctor may check your ___.

   coat   throat   pocket

5. A seatbelt will ___ you in a crash.

   inspect   eject   protect

fact, tears, talk, throat, protect

Circle the vowel team that is in the word for the picture.

1.

ai   oa

5.

ie   ee

2.

ue   ie

6.

ea   ie

3.

ee   ai

7.

oa   ai

4.

ea   ie

8.

ee   ai

nail, tie, tree, peach, green, pie, goat, tail

Review
Write the words for each picture.

1.

_____
- -
_____

2.

_____
- -
_____

3.

_____
- -
_____

4.

_____
- -
_____

5.

_____
- -
_____

6.

_____
- -
_____

saw, rain, goat, cloud, roll, fly

Review
Unscramble the words to make a sentence.
Remember: the first letter in the first word gets
capitalized, and don't forget the period.

jump   likes

girl   rope   to   the

1) _____

_ _

_____

_ _

The girl likes to jump rope.

plays   boy

in   the

the   sand

2) _____

_ _

_____

_ _

The boy plays in the sand.

Read the sentence and circle the word that makes sense.

1. The sick man is not strong, he is weak / tall.

2. When we sleep, we have hotdogs / dreams.

3. The mean fish / lady will yell at you.

4. We listen with our feet / ears.

5. The sun makes lots of corn / heat.

6. Jim took his boat out to fish / sleep.

weak, dreams, lady, ears, heat, fish

Review

Read the words below.

acting	draw	soon
fact	drew	sooner
actress	new	helper

collect - collecting

swim - swimming

drink - drinking

think - thinking

Fill in the missing letters.

 Conn __ __ __
the dots.

Remember our vowel teams?

ai ee ea ie oa ue

'ea' can have a short e' sound.

In this lesson, we see that 'ea' can have a **short 'e' sound**, instead of a long 'e' sound.

ea = /eh/ as in "elephant".

Since this breaks our long vowel rule, we call this sound a "rule breaker".

Listed below are the **most common** 'ea' words.

head	sweat	ready
dead	sweater	steady
dread	weather	heavy
bread	feather	instead

Draw lines to match the words to their pictures.

Remember: ea can sound like /eh/ as in "elephant".

1. w<u>ea</u>lthy

2. f<u>ea</u>thers

3. br<u>ea</u>d

4. sw<u>ea</u>ter

5. h<u>ea</u>ven

6. thr<u>ea</u>d

bread, thread, feathers, wealthy, sweater, heaven

Circle the picture that goes with the sentence.

1. If it is cold outside, put on a sw<u>ea</u>ter.

2. The w<u>ea</u>lthy man threw money into the air.

3. The dog has bad br<u>ea</u>th.

4. Inst<u>ea</u>d of flying, I will take the train.

5. The doctor will check your h<u>ea</u>lth.

Circle the correct word for each sentence.

1. To sew, we use a needle and <u>thread / tree</u>.

2. When will you be <u>steady / ready</u> to go?

3. Your neck holds up your <u>leg / head</u>.

4. If the bug is not alive, it is <u>wealthy / dead</u>.

5. The boxes are too <u>heavy / brown</u> to lift.

thread, ready, head, dead, heavy.

Read the story below.

Last week, I went to the park.

I sat under the tree and read a book.

The sun was very hot.

I took off my sweater. I wiped the sweat

from my forehead.

Just then a big, heavy dog ran up to me.

He leapt up onto my lap. He had bad breath.

I held my nose, and I gave him a big hug.

Review
Fill in the missing letters for the words.

1. sn ☐ k ☐

2. ch ☐☐ t

3. c ☐☐ ch

4. str ☐☐

5. scr ☐☐☐☐

6. d ☐☐☐ or

snake, chart, couch, straw, scratch, doctor

Review
Fill in the missing letters for the words.

1. m☐☐th

2. sp☐☐n

3. br☐☐d

4. ☐☐☐or

5. cr☐☐

6. sl☐☐p

mouth, spoon, bread, actor, crow, sleep

Read the clue, then choose the word. You will have
to change the word so that it makes sense.
Write the new words on the lines.

ing

1. The boy is

read   point

_____

2. The child is

draw   talk

_____

3. The bee is

string   sting

_____

4. The woman is

sleep   think

_____

reading, drawing, stinging, thinking

Review
Unscramble the words to make a sentence.
Remember: the first letter in the first word gets capitalized, and don't forget the period.

blew   the

kite   wind   my

1)

_____

- -

_____

_____

- -

_____

The wind blew my kite.

read   girl

at   her

the   desk

2)

_____

- -

_____

_____

- -

_____

The girl read at her desk.

Review

Read the words below.

bread	ready	claw
head	instead	pause
dead	threat	walk
death	heavy	chalk

connect - connecting

inspect - inspecting

Fill in the missing letters.

sw __ __ ter   h __ __ d

In the past lessons, you have
been adding 'ing' to many words.
For example:

drink - drink<u>ing</u>

sleep - sleep<u>ing</u>

But what about words with short vowels?

swim - swiming ✕

Oh no! Our fairy just turned the 'i' long!
To keep this from happening we double
the consonant (in this case 'm') to protect
the short vowel (in this case 'i').

swim - swi<u>mm</u>ing

Double the consonant
to protect the short
vowel.

You can think of the two consonants as being bodyguards, who protect the short vowel.

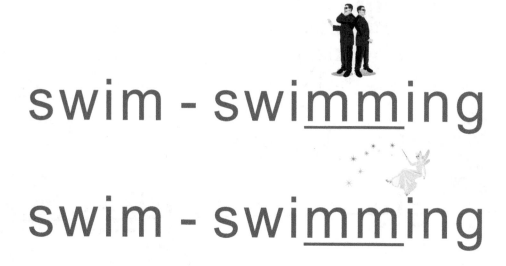

swim - swi<u>mm</u>ing

swim - swi<u>mm</u>ing

And now the magic fairy dust won't reach the vowel.

run - ru<u>nn</u>ing

skip - sk<u>ipp</u>ing

bat - ba<u>tt</u>ing

slam - sla<u>mm</u>ing

* Sounds like 'oo' and 'oi' are not short vowels
and do <u>not</u> need to be protected.

sh<u>oo</u>t - sh<u>oo</u>ting

b<u>oi</u>l - b<u>oi</u>ling

Read the words below out loud. When adding 'ing', did
we have to **double a consonant** to protect a short vowel?

yes   no

		yes	no
1.	sip	sipping	✔	
2.	scoot	scooting		
3.	throw	throwing		
4.	pat	patting		
5.	bump	bumping		
6.	clap	clapping		

1) yes, 2) no, 3) no, 4) yes, 5) no, 6) yes

In some words, consonants are
already doubled to protect short vowels.
*Remember, 'y' can act like a vowel, so it can turn
another vowel long*. Read the words below.

bu<u>tt</u>er

da<u>dd</u>y

bu<u>nn</u>y

mo<u>mm</u>y

Circle the consonants (bodyguards) that are protecting
a short vowel. Then read the words out loud.

1. gu(tt)er

2. better

3. matter

4. funny

5. happy

6. fussy

Add 'ing' to the following words.
* Don't forget to protect the short vowels.*

1. get   getting

2. sip

3. cut

4. run

5. sit

getting, sipping cutting, running, sitting

Read the passage below.

When it is cold outside, I must dress warm.

First I will put on a sweater. Then I will

put on my coat. To keep my neck warm,

I will wear a scarf. To keep my hands warm,

I will wear my mittens. To keep my feet warm

I will wear thick socks and boots. To keep

my head warm, I will wear a hat.

Can you name the missing item?

The missing item is the hat.

Read the sentences and **circle** the words that have consonants (bodyguards) protecting short vowels.

1. She is sitting on the stool.

2. Liz is sipping her drink.

3. We were getting ready to go out.

4. The maid was mopping the floor.

5. We were planning to see the show.

6. The cook was flipping pancakes.

sitting, sipping, getting, mopping, planning, flipping

Adding 'er' to a Word

When you add other endings that start with vowels, such as 'er, you will still have to
double the consonants to protect short vowels.
For example:

sit - si<u>tt</u>er

win - wi<u>nn</u>er

hug - hu<u>gg</u>er

You need **two** bodyguards
to protect the short vowel.

Now my fairy dust will not
reach the short vowel.

Add 'er' to the following words.
Don't forget to protect the short vowel.

1. red   r e d d e r

2. quit

3. spin

4. big

5. fat

redder, quitter, spinner, bigger, fatter

Read the sentences and fill in the missing letters for the words. Remember to protect the short vowels.

1. It gets ho___ ___er in the summer.

   hot

2. She is si___ ___ing her drink.

   sip

3. They were cla___ ___ing their hands.

   clap

4. The cat was ru___ ___ing away from me.

   run

5. The rabbit was ho___ ___ing down the hill.

   hop

bigger   smaller

hotter, sipping, clapping, running, hopping

Circle the picture that goes with the sentence.

Spread the butter on the bread.

The boy is a winner!

We will have turkey for dinner.

The lady is a fast runner.

Review
The frog only likes to eat words where the 'ea' is a short 'e'
sound. Circle the words that have the short 'e' sound,
(there are 4).

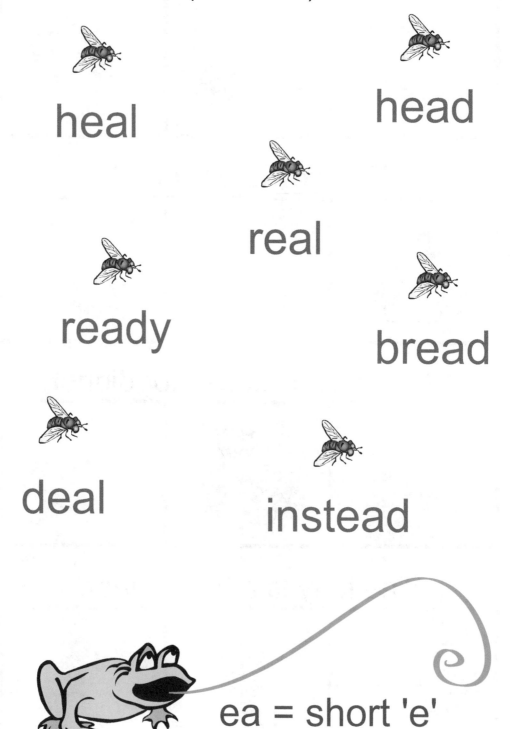

heal

head

real

ready

bread

deal

instead

ea = short 'e'

head, ready, bread, instead

Review
Unscramble the words to make a sentence.
Remember: the first letter in the first word gets
capitalized, and don't forget the period.

pushing   lady   the

is   the   chair

1) _____

_____

_____

_____

The lady is pushing the chair.

is   she   the

bread   cutting

2) _____

_____

_____

She is cutting the bread.

Review

Read the words below.

run - runner - running

spin - spinner - spinning

quit - quitter - quitting

hit - hitter - hitting

roll - roller - rolling

stick - sticker - sticking

Fill in the missing letters and read the words.

h___ ___ven

f ___ ___ thers

heaven, feathers

Past Tense Words

Review flash cards.

Often when reading, you are reading about something that already happened. That means you are reading in the **past tense**. Past tense words usually have 'ed' at the end, but some past tense words are special and do **not** get the 'ed' added at the end.

Below are some **special** words that change when they are past tense.

drink - drank

run - ran

sit - sat

Below are word that get the 'ed' added for past tense.

fold<u>ed</u>

jump<u>ed</u>

shout<u>ed</u>

You usually know a past tense word when you hear it.
If you have trouble, use the sentences below and
fill in the blanks with the word.

Today I _____.

Yesterday I _____.

Read the words below and then say the word as
past tense. Use the sentences above if you need to.

clap   walk

win   bake

smell   list

Today I swim, but
yesterday I swam!

When you are writing a past tense word that is NOT special (like "eat" and "ate" and "drink" and "drank) then you MUST add the 'ed' -
EVEN IF YOU DON'T HEAR IT.

And

You may have to double a consonant to protect a short vowel.

plan - pla<u>nn</u>ed

* Add 'ed' even though you may not hear /ed/ *

IF you spell the word the way it sounds you may be falling into the past tense trap!

Past Tense
Trap

pland

Circle the picture that goes with the word.

1. scrubbed

2. spilled

3. licked

4. yelled

5. tossed

6. dressed

Circle the past tense word that is correctly spelled.

1. shop ➡ shopt   shopped

2. kick ➡ kicked   kict

3. pack ➡ pact   packed

4. turn ➡ turnd   turned

5. lick ➡ licked   lict

6. plan ➡ planned   pland

Watch out for the past tense trap!

shopped, kicked, packed, turned, licked, planned

Make the following words past tense.
Use the sentences: "Today I __. Yesterday I __."

+ ed

1. play

2. rain

3. yawn

Remember to protect your short vowel.

4. clap

5. clean

There is something very strange for the past tense words that get the 'ed' added to the end. Sometimes you don't hear the 'ed' and instead you hear a /t/ or /d/ sound!

Read the words below to your student.

jump - jump<u>ed</u>

rain - rain<u>ed</u>

wish - wish<u>ed</u>

crash - crash<u>ed</u>

* Notice how all the words we just read sound like they end with a /t/ or /d/ sound.

In the words below, you **do** hear the 'ed'.

last - last<u>ed</u>

rest - rest<u>ed</u>

hand - hand<u>ed</u>

list - list<u>ed</u>

> To make a word, with 'e' at the end,
> past tense, just add the 'd'.
>
> # tim<u>e</u> - tim<u>ed</u>

Read the sentences and make the missing words past tense.

1. Today I <u>smile</u>, but yesterday I _____.

_____

_____

2. Today I <u>rake</u>, but yesterday I _____.

_____

_____

3. Today I <u>bake</u>, but yesterday I _____.

_____

_____

4. Today I <u>hike</u>, but yesterday I _____.

_____

_____

smiled, raked, baked, hiked

Read the passage below.

Ashley pitched the ball. The batter hit the ball and then ran. She ran around all of the bases. She skidded into the home plate. The score was tied. Ashley did not want the other team to score. She held her breath and pitched the ball to the next batter. The batter swung and missed the ball. This happened two more times. Three strikes means you are out! The game was over. Ashley's team won!

Review
Unscramble the words to make a sentence.
Remember: the first letter in the first word gets
capitalized, and don't forget the period.

pushed lady the

the chair

1)

_____

- -

_____

_____

- -

_____

The lady pushed the chair.

birthday  a cake

baked Grandma

2)

_____

- -

_____

_____

- -

_____

Grandma baked a birthday cake.

Review

Read the words below.

blast-blasted   dress-dressed

last-lasted   talk-talked

test-tested   fold-folded

Read and trace the sentence, filling in the missing word.

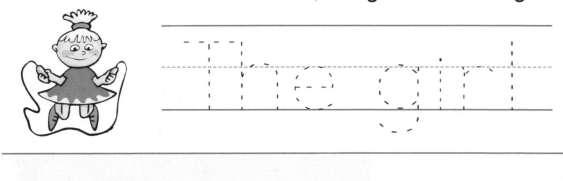

The girl

over

the rope.

Continue to review the flash cards, play the online games, and have your child read to you. You may want to proceed to *Blast Off to Reading!*, which will review what was taught here and teach more sounds and rules.

CPSIA information can be obtained
at www.ICGtesting.com
Printed in the USA
BVHW062214250721
612621BV00008B/64